DEFENSES

Bloody HORNED LIZARDS

by Lori Haskins Houran

Consultant: Gabrielle Sachs
Zoo Educator

BEARPORT PUBLISHING

NEW YORK, NEW YORK

Credits

Cover, © John Cancalosi/Alamy; TOC, © Rusty Dodson/Shutterstock; 4, © Ellen McKnight/Alamy; 5, © Raymond Mendez/Animals Animals-Earth Scenes; 6, © John Cancalosi/ardea.com; 7, © Wade C. Sherbrooke, Ph.D.; 8, © Raymond Mendez/Animals Animals-Earth Scenes; 9, © Wade C. Sherbrooke, Ph.D.; 10, © Wade C. Sherbrooke, Ph.D.; 11, © John A.L. Cooke/Animals Animals-Earth Scenes; 12, © Wade C. Sherbrooke, Ph.D.; 13, © John Cancalosi/Peter Arnold; 14, © Ralph A. Clevenger/Corbis; 15, © Barry Mansell/Minden Pictures; 16, © Wade C. Sherbrooke, Ph.D.; 17, © Joe McDonald/Tom Stack & Associates; 18, © Wade C. Sherbrooke, Ph.D.; 19, © Wade C. Sherbrooke, Ph.D.; 20, © Tom Grundy/Shutterstock; 21, © McDonald Wildlife Photography/Animals Animals-Earth Scenes; 22, © Dr. Morley Read/Photo Researchers, Inc.; 23TL, © Wade C. Sherbrooke, Ph.D.; 23TR, © Joe McDonald/Tom Stack & Associates; 23BL, © Wade C. Sherbrooke, Ph.D.; 23BR, © Wade C. Sherbrooke, Ph.D.

Publisher: Kenn Goin
Senior Editor: Lisa Wiseman
Creative Director: Spencer Brinker
Design: Becky Munich
Photo Researcher: Amy Dunleavy

Library of Congress Cataloging-in-Publication Data

Haskins, Lori.
  Bloody horned lizards / by Lori Haskins Houran.
     p. cm. — (Gross-out defenses)
  Includes bibliographical references and index.
  ISBN-13: 978-1-59716-717-8 (library binding)
  ISBN-10: 1-59716-717-7 (library binding)
  1. Horned toads— Juvenile literature. 2. Animal defenses— Juvenile literature. I. Title.

  QL666.L267H37 2009
  597.95'4— dc22

                    2008016048

For more information, write to Bearport Publishing Company, Inc., 101 Fifth Avenue, Suite 6R, New York, New York 10003. Printed in the United States of America.

10 9 8 7 6 5 4 3 2 1

Contents

Surprise!

Uh-oh! A horned lizard sees trouble.

A hungry coyote is coming near.

Closer, closer . . .

The lizard shuts its eyes tight, then—
squirt!

It shoots blood out of its eyes, straight into the coyote's mouth!

The shocked coyote yelps and turns away.

The lizard is safe!

coyote

Shooting blood is a weird way to fight off **enemies,** but it works! Horned lizards spray the blood out of the corners of their eyes. If they need to, they can shoot over and over again.

shooting blood

Unlucky Dogs

Horned lizards don't squirt blood at just anyone.

They save this trick for **canine** enemies, such as coyotes, foxes, wolves, and dogs.

The lizards' blood tastes horrible to these creatures, though it doesn't bother other kinds of animals at all.

The blood doesn't hurt the canines. It just grosses them out! After they're squirted, canines shake their heads and rub their faces in the grass, trying to get rid of the terrible taste.

Good Shot

How does a horned lizard shoot blood from its eyes?

It squeezes special muscles that store blood in its head.

The blood builds up until it finally bursts out of the corners of the lizard's eyes.

The lizard can aim the blood forward or backward, hitting enemies up to four feet (1.2 m) away!

There are more than a dozen different types of horned lizards. Some kinds don't shoot blood—or at least no one has ever seen them do it!

eye filled with blood

Lots of Tricks

Blood-squirting is just one of the weird ways that horned lizards protect themselves.

Sometimes they gulp air into their bodies and blow up like balloons!

They do this so they'll look too big for enemies to swallow.

Lizards also flatten themselves like pancakes.

Why? So birds won't see their shadows from the sky.

If nothing else works, horned lizards try to scare enemies away. They stand up on their back legs, open their mouths, and hiss like a snake!

Ouch!

Why would any animal want to eat a horned lizard?

It doesn't look very tasty.

Its body is covered with hard scales and prickly spines.

It has super-sharp horns on its head.

Yet snakes, roadrunners, and hawks all hunt horned lizards.

roadrunner

Sometimes a snake tries to swallow a lizard, but the lizard is too big and gets stuck in its throat. The lizard's horns poke through the snake's skin, killing it in the middle of its meal.

horns

spines

scales

Revenge of the Ants

One of the lizard's enemies is also its favorite food.

A horned lizard eats hundreds of ants a day, gulping them down whole.

Yum!

However, if enough ants gang up against a lizard, they can sting it to death.

ants

tongue

Horned lizards flick out their tongues to catch ants. They look like toads when they do this, which is one reason they're nicknamed "horny toads."

Hide and Seek

North America is the only place horned lizards live.

They're found mostly in desert areas, though they're very hard to spot.

Lizards have skin that blends in with the rocks and sand.

This **camouflage** is yet another way they keep themselves safe from enemies.

radio transmitter

Sometimes scientists strap tiny radio transmitters onto the backs of horned lizards. The radios send signals that tell the scientists where the lizards are hiding.

NORTH AMERICA

ATLANTIC OCEAN

PACIFIC OCEAN

SOUTH AMERICA

N
W · E
S

☐ Where horned lizards live

Digging In

Horned lizards spend a lot of time underground.

They dig **burrows** in the soil where they can warm up at night and cool down during the day.

Mother lizards lay their eggs in burrows, too.

Then they leave their eggs—and don't come back.

Luckily, baby lizards can take care of themselves right after they hatch.

eggs

burrow

Some kinds of
horned lizards don't
lay eggs. Instead, the
mothers give birth to
live young.

Tiny But Tough

Baby horned lizards are no bigger than a thumbtack.

Even full-grown lizards are only about five inches (13 cm) long.

It's hard to believe these tiny creatures can fight off a wolf with nothing more than a squirt of blood!

baby horned lizard

Long ago, some
people believed that
horned lizards could cure
sickness, make it rain,
or even bring good luck!
Lizards don't really have
these powers, but they're
still amazing animals.

21

Another Gross Defense

Horned lizards aren't the only animals that squirt gross stuff. Velvet worms spit a gluey slime at their enemies—up to 12 inches (30 cm) away! They also use it to catch spiders, crickets, and termites. The slime hardens around these creatures, and then the worms eat them—slime and all!

Glossary

burrows
(BUR-ohz) holes in the ground where horned lizards live

camouflage
(KAM-uh-flahzh) disguising oneself through fur or skin to blend into one's surroundings

canine
(KAY-nine) an animal that is a member of the dog family

enemies
(EN-uh-meez) animals that hunt other animals for survival

23

Index

Read More

Glaser, Jason. *Horned Lizards*. Mankato, MN: Capstone Press (2006).

Schaefer, Lola M. *Horned Toads*. Chicago: Heinemann Library (2004).

Trueit, Trudi Strain. *Lizards*. New York: Children's Press (2003).

Learn More Online

To learn more about horned lizards, visit
www.bearportpublishing.com/GrossOutDefenses

About the Author

Lori Haskins Houran has been writing and editing books since 1992. She lives in New York City.